Word and Stone

For Norman & Deborah
with love
Jerry

Jeremy Hooker

Word and Stone

Shearsman Books

First published in the United Kingdom in 2019 by
Shearsman Books
50 Westons Hill Drive
Emersons Green
BRISTOL
BS16 7DF

Shearsman Books Ltd Registered Office
30–31 St. James Place, Mangotsfield, Bristol BS16 9JB
(this address not for correspondence)

www.shearsman.com

ISBN 978-1-84861-672-1

Contents

To Mieke
with me always

Word and Stone

'Ye also, as lively stones, are built up
a spiritual house…'
                    1 Peter 2:5

'… the sculptor shapes only the stone,
the dead stone, and the poet only the word,
which in itself is dead. But the statesman
shapes the masses …'
                    Joseph Goebbels, May 1933

1
A carved hand
holding a cross
is cut in the castle floor.

Under the floor
crushed skulls
mix with bloodstained soil.

Outside
the sea shifts
breaking and making
          for ever.

2
The cross cut in stone
states what it is:

foundation,
word written in rock.

It has fronted the sea
for centuries
slowly wearing away.

3
Before word
there was a cry,
a breath against the stone.

It takes a hand of flint
to write in rock.

A strong hand
scattering sparks
striking down.

The word settles in

making itself a home –
a house of spirit

a field of skulls.

4
Before words
there was stone.

Before stone,
water and fire.

Creatures
looked up from the sea.

Their wordless cry
lives in us until we die.

5
Men took up stones
to build a castle.

Other men came to bless it,
perhaps this man –
who may have been gentle –
with the carved hand.

Who asked the women
what they wanted?

They bow down
as they are bid
and kiss the stone.

6
Words in the mouths
of men with power
round the world,

        crushing it

like an apple in the fist.

7
Masterful words,
with the might
of clenched hands –

which strike at the roots
scattering pith and sap,
sundering limb from limb.

But always a sense
beyond the sense
survives:

an apple on the branch
beyond the grasp of words.

8
The image wearing away
wants to break free.

It longs to become
a word with spirit.

It beats against
castle walls.

It cracks
the shell of the skull.

It desires to fly
as gulls fly

out to sea
to settle on the deep.

9
The great stones
move in their own world
which men and women
approach fearfully

daubing with blood

listening
           waiting
for the stone

the stranger

the blank-faced one

to speak.

10
This is the way of words

The cursus leads to the ring.
Dawn with a spear of light
strikes through cloud.

All paths lead down
over cobble skulls
through tangled roots
                    into the earth.

11
Beyond the smashed teeth,
the bloody pulp,
the gouged mouths

among the corpses
a live word

gasps

thirsting

to speak again.

12
The antique castle will fall,
the carved hand drown
in shingle and wrack.

Words like gulls
will scream on the deep

crying

with endless discontent
of what may be.

Skylarks, cromlechs

for Christopher Meredith

You open the car door, and I step out
onto rough moorland grass,
                                        at my feet
the tiny yellow faces of tormentil,
and young bracken,
tender curling fronds renewing
earth wasted by last year's harvest,
and stretching far, from hill
to wraiths of higher, blue-domed hills.
Most wonderful, after weeks indoors
watching the sky through windows,
the wind in my face,
                                  a touch
that wakes the sleeper to the world.
Far off, the Beacons climb into cloud,
massive rounded blue-grey forms.
All is shadow, and substance,
                                        and song –
skylarks quivering as they fly up,
rising, rising, pouring
their voices over the earth,
into the wind that carries the sounds away.
As we move on, passing
broken ground, with groups of fallen stones,
I think: How could anyone not wish to be here.
Ancient ones,
voiceless generations,
                              it is all becoming
moment-to-moment:
lark song pouring down,
Beacons climbing into cloud,
young bracken unfurling
under the touch of the wind.

Welsh chapel in winter

Windows of the chapel house
look out on a cold country
half buried in snow.

Zion is blind; no one
worships here now.

Sheep huddle
against a stone wall.
The one human presence,
pylons, in steely light,
draw power-lines
over valley and hill.

Preacher, visionary,
people from hill farm
and pit village
have passed this way
and gone, deepening
the isolation.

No one comes here
unless, on some day in summer,
a solitary visitor
or a family, seeking
grandparents among the graves.

The very silence
is like a cry, or echo
of a fragment
of sermon or song,
voices that rise and vanish
into the strange land.

Pictures at an Exhibition

(*Engaging with the Past,*
Oriel y Bont, Tŷ Crawshay)

1
This woman
who has a landscape behind her,
this monumental figure
in shawl and chimney hat,
what shall we call her?

Lady of Wales in the rain,
of lead sky and coal-black hills,
or a revival of a revival,
a painted maiden
from a time that never was?

How demure she seems,
her face pretty as a primrose.

But look at her mouth
and shadowed eyes,
her smile that no man can read.

2
What shall we do? they ask.
We are men beggared and blind.
We are thieves with stolen lives.

We are men in a place that does not own us,
clowns looking for a part in an empty theatre.

This land is not our fathers' or our mothers',
but our children's,
who totter in our broken steps.

Land of the black heart
under the green hills,
once the wealth of empire,
now the land called Bugger All.

3
Look at me, she says.
Do you think me an illusion
that you painted in your mind?

Do you suppose me
a silly story of flowers
and a witless owl?

Though you stand at your easel
for ever, I do not submit to be known.

This imagined flesh
pure as sea-washed shell
is stuff that's come out of the sea,

moon-driven,
fierce as the tides.

I will make of myself what I will.
You, I will leave to your dream.

Llantwit Major: the Celtic Stones

Time lies heavy on their shoulders,
these ancient ones.

Illtud, Samson, Huellt
who prepared a cross
for the soul of his father.

Under the electric light,
in the restored chapel,
shadow weighs them down.

But this is illusion.
They are peregrini
who abandoned time,
pilgrims on broken Roman roads,
missionaries who gave their coracles
to the mercy of the Maker of the tides.

What they left to ages of darkness
was an image of time, turned to stone.

Daffodil, magpies, fir

One light the storm

could not put out –

a daffodil

rain has pelted, winds blasted

as they have lashed the fir

close by – an elastic tree

in which magpies building

have held on, or, venturing out

been blown about the sky

while I have watched, admiring

flower and tree and birds

wishing to have, like them,

power to spring back, endure.

The Green Woodpecker

There is nostalgia
that draws me back
into the mire, and there is love
that liberates.

So I call on you to guide me
bird of the laughing call
greenback, redhead
with yellow rump.

How laboured
your flight seems,
looping from grove to glade
anthill to anthill
as if you would fall.

Did you fly into the painted cave
or out of it – bird
on a stick in the shaman's hand?

Old one, you were always
most at home on the ground
beak ploughing
for larvae and ants.

        Yet nostalgia
also can be an energy –
memory a flight
that gives wings to the mind.

        My father
was a gardener and a painter
but no bird-man.

Once, in the greenhouse
he found, wings beating
wildly among the tomatoes
in peaty warmth
what he thought a parrot.

And indeed there is
something exotic
about you, native bird.

Yaffle,
yaffingale
of ancient times
woodpecker
'who also is Zeus'

rain-bird
thunder-spirit
from how far back
you fly into our world.

From glade to grove,
from anthill to anthill,
you fly –
no drummer of dead wood
but a bird with a beak
for digging, a soil-grubber
since Mars was a farmer.

And why do I call you now,
in age the boy I was
relishing my short time,
laughing one,
greenback in the green wood?

Here I come
with scratched legs

from heath to cover
of the ancient trees,
and there you are
looping from glade to grove

as if you would fall.

Blackthorn and Celandine

Anticipation's the word.

Snatches of song from birds
remembering to sing,
voices coming back…
Pairings, skirmishes –
a new thought in wintry air,
a spirit waking.

I wait for the first white tuft,
a snowflake of flower
on the black bough,
a feathering
before the touch of green.
I look in ditch and on hedge-bank
for a yellow star,
first of a constellation.

And now there's no sign,
only a feeling, a memory.

Other years pile up,
leaves on leaves, a mould
that accumulates,
a weight on the heart,
a burden on the mind.

And what is this
but something to grow in,
compost for a green shoot?

'Old man', you say,
surprised, as if coming awake.

You think of the world
you have not changed;
you dream of the lives
you've dreamed of,
possibilities unrealised;
you see the very globe,
the folly of the kind you are.

And so you wait, watching
for the first white tuft
against the black bough,
anticipating the first yellow star.

What's new, old man?

It's always the same,
this newness,
and you are ever in love with it,

eager for what may come.

Aneurin Bevan Memorial Stones

1

Limestone was his rock
at Trefil, on Llangynidr mountain,
on paths to the Chartists' Cave,
a dark mouth opening on a darker history,
articulate with the silence that filled it.

The stonechat heard him
and the ring ouzel among the rocks,
this young man with a stutter
declaiming Shakespeare or Marx,
correcting his voice, and honing it,
like a tool, useful as a miner's pick.

2

His story is like an old myth
in a land of myth –
this monolith that was a man,
a boulder from the quarry where he walked,
and round him, three smaller stones,
his constituents, like petrified dancers,
the people he spoke to –
Ebbw Vale, Tredegar, Rhymney,
and, beyond them, the world.

3

It is like a tale that begins
with poverty and ends with power:

Butcher's boy, miner, Minister
of State – one man
learning to speak for the people

he came from – miners,
steelworkers, families,
honing a tongue to bristle
and condemn, a voice with power to probe
the narrow privacies, and erode
the obdurate rock that is privilege.

4

Limestone was his rock,
organic, soluble stuff, material
to shape a new world.

He would quote William Morris:
Fellowship is life
and lack of fellowship is death.

Man of flesh become stone,
this could not be a story that has an end.

The rock flakes away; the voice still speaks.

In the Lloyd George Museum

1

In one photograph
a dark-haired poet looks up.
He is proud, perhaps defiant, his arms
laid on the arms of the bardic chair.

He is being honoured
by principalities and powers,
and perhaps humoured,
for the Statesman who stands beside him,
playing his part, wears a slight smile.

It amazes me to recognise the poet,
who is still young.

I saw him in old age,
the skull showing in his face
which was like parchment
where feeling had written
the history of his people.

The dead, brown leaves
of the laurel wreath were not his.
It was thrown into the carriage
in which the Statesman drove
through London, with the King,
returning in triumph
from Versailles.

Surely there are materials here
for a poem about history:
fifty years of cartoons
and newspaper photographs –
manhandled suffragettes

with the clothes clawed off their backs,
munitions, wars, faces.

2

How could I understand?

It was fifty years ago when I saw him.
I was young,
and new to the Wales that had made him.
He was on the far side of another language.

What I saw was a face I could not read,
where death showed in the brow,
the sockets of the eyes.

But it wasn't death he spoke of,
this small man, consumed
by the fury that fed him.

Call it life, but not a life that I knew:
the coffin smell in parlours,
the corpse of his father
burnt in a fall of molten steel,
the ancestral home
alive with humour and humanity
and ancient song, gone
to a pile of rubble
under a forest of sterile pines,
all power in the hands of builders
of machines of war and makers
of monuments of dross,
children lost, a generation
asphyxiated in a tide of industrial filth.

On the road from Moscow to Calfaria
no word would suffice for this poet
who sounded the new day with an ancient tongue.

No word but the starkest,
drawn from a land sown
with bones and dust of saints.
A word scoured of illusion,
and among the countless faces,
one face – the man-god
who went down with men into the pit,
who stood with them in the heat of the furnace,
the one who is guest and host
in places where no man can go
and the only other visitor is death.

On the eve of my seventy-fifth year

1
Tiny green leaves
on the crab-apple
and a west wind bringing rain.

I see my grandfather
with his young family
proud at the wheel
of an antique car
which was the latest model.

2
Rain dimples the window
bare branches knock together.

My older brother
who died young
is lying beside me
in our bedroom, joking,
making me laugh
at RAF slang.

Who, when I die,
will remember his ways?

3
Old fool, these
are signs of age,
wanderings
on borders of the mind.

Better to watch
the black branches
before they blossom.

Better to see, with pleasure,
the raindrops
and tiny green leaves.

Chloe

With an ocean between us,
that day when you opened your eyes
for the first time, I heard
a cardinal singing his love song
in the April woods.

Your father's voice on the phone
was wondering, tender, as he told me
how you turned from purple to pink
in his arms, and opened your eyes.

Chloe, I thought:
a young herb, a green shoot.
In the upstate woods
plants were pushing aside dead leaves,
and the bird was singing, as though
to whistle up the grass and flowers.

Lines for the poet at seven years of age

for Harry Jeremy, my grandson

This is the way to begin,
with wonder at yourself –
I AM – and wonder
at all that has made you:
family and friends,
cities and countries…
Already, in your words,
I see your travels, and hear you
playing at school and in the park.
I see, too, a mind quick with questions.
Is there life on other stars?
Will a black hole swallow us?

I delight in your delight,
and feel, yes, a little envy.
You, too, may face
the temptation, which is
a poet's special curse.
And an old man's who
is tempted also to advise,
and cannot help himself…

What I dare say is this:
if you write, it will be
an old faith you live by.
You will write it all – slant
or direct, but with a voice
that is yours
and not yours alone,
your human voice.
This wonder is where you begin.

Blank days will come,
days, it seems, that are ages
when the poet you dreamed
you were is self-sick, a man
without a tongue, wordless
or with words dead on the page.

This is the time to let
the winter of metaphor
come – the frost, the blank
fields of snow, eternal
December's grey sky
heavy on mind and heart.

This door you have pushed open
is the Janus face of art.
On one side the bleak fields.
On the other an uncertain
tender ripening, or pursuit –
it is all metaphor –
of what must escape,
but leave in your hands a sign.

Each time it will be time
to start again, believing what has been
will return, but never the same.

Listen, and you will hear
the dead alive in your song.

To M. in her sickness

'...a human being is like a half-fragment'

From the hospital
a nurse rings to tell me
you are 'holding your own'.

I look out,
watching a small cloud
shaped like a rowing boat
crossing the blue sky
of an April day.

As I watch
the cloud-boat founders
leaving the sky empty.

Oh, my dear, what if we too
should break apart!

How inadequate my words
freighted with all I cannot say

Greenfinches

Convalescing,
you stood by the window
delighting to watch them –
parent birds flying
from tree to garden hedge,
fledglings trembling
on the verge of flight.

How free they seemed –
quick-winged, filling the air
with moss-green,
a flash of yellow,
a dash of song.

How they flourish,
you thought, how free –
until this:
two young ones
dead, necks broken
against the glass.

Here, at this big window,
which lets in the light,
the healing light, where
you have looked out, feeling
on imprisoning days something
within you that could almost fly.

St Mary's, Kempley: The Wheel of Life

Exhausted by the walk from the car,
I lean on my trusty NHS stick.
It is an old story that I step into:
seraphim and apostles, the Last Judgement,
Christ seated on a rainbow.
A monk's vision in earth colours
of the whole creation, poised
between Heaven and Hell.

Outside, the village has moved away.
Fields recede towards the Malverns.
Piers Plowman might have worshipped here.

Two pilgrims with staffs,
father and son, appear between the windows.
The father, Baron Walter de Lacy,
fought at the Battle of Hastings.
His son built the church
and commissioned the paintings
in his father's memory.
And here they are, together,
humbled, on the way
to the heavenly Jerusalem.

Turning from image to image,
I am stunned by The Wheel of Life.
Here is the child I was, sitting
rub a dub dub on my mother's knee
before the fire. The young man
with a hawk on his wrist
riding a white horse into the fields –
he might have been me in another age.
Now I am the elderly man
pictured leaning on his staff.

And so the wheel turns
spoke by spoke –
as men and women
weary from the fields
would have seen, seated here
age after age, generation
after generation, resting
their aching limbs, held
in a monk's vision, pilgrims
from these fields, dreading
and dreaming of another world.

Wood Fidley Rain

for Robert Macfarlane

1
How did it differ, I wonder,
from mizzle that pearls
spider-webs on the heath
and dints rivers and ponds
or rain ordinarily falling
on the forest canopy
and dripping down the trees?

They said it could be seen
on the way, in a special light
behind the beeches on the ridge.

And when it came it fell
day-long, night-long, drenching
all who sought the scant protection
of the understorey and the trees.

2
Close by a bishop crawling
on his belly for perhaps a mile –
as we used to say –
round heath and bog
would have looked up
fearfully as he made his claim
to land – more land – and left
his name attached to ditch
and dyke and purlieu –
a wild place which
he coveted for snipe
that nested on the marshy ground.

3
They're all long-gone,
those who saw the light
beyond Woodfidley
and heard the wind whistle –
hooi hooi – the trees
scroop and the gloxing water.

Bishop and woodmen,
all who cared for the vert
and the venison, commoners,
man, woman and child –
all who looked up to Woodfidley
and saw the light that brought the rain.

All gone, and nothing to speak
of them except an old book
and words they tasted
on their tongues, like rain.

Frosted Forest

On a birthday card from my daughter

I know these mornings,
how cold they are, how warm the colours:

heather blue as an unshaved jaw,
sunlit bracken with red-gold flame.

I know that Scot's pine, a solitary
on the heath, crown
turned from the sea,
trunk and branches scaly
as a prehistoric lizard.

It too is a denizen of *Nova Foresta*.
It belongs as much as woodlands
of oak and beech.
It too remembers the cry of hounds
chasing the king's deer.

So let it stand now
as it does in this picture
for all the trees of the Forest.

Let it be today, as you wish, my tree.

Found: Wordsworth on epitaphs

1
Where the river Rothay flows,
beside the churchyard wall,
a child stands pondering.

Down from crags and fells,
the Rothay flows, fast falling,
gathering tributaries – beck & burn & ghyll –
in spate, it drowns the stepping stones.

The boy sees ripples,
flashes, rocks with flying capes –
sparks from darting light,
round shouldered heaving ridge
dissolving and new formed,
one body breaking as it flows:
Companion river! Puzzle to the end!
It is a language that he reads,
a world of watery words,
some ever passing spirit that remains,
a composition in his mind.

2
Down from crags and fells,
close by the churchyard wall,
the river Rothay glides.

Behind the wall, beside
the plot of grass and yews,
one stone among the family
of graves stands out:
Wordsworth the poet
here has made his final choice.

No verse to trifle with remains,
no word injurious to the human heart,
but, simple as the air we breathe,
his name,
a tribute to the common earth.

St Laurence's, Bradford on Avon

Rediscovered, it opened
upon a world we can scarcely imagine,
with rumours of martyrs
and Saxon kings
and a master of Latin verse.

But here it is:
a narrow room under a high roof,
with barely enough light
to see the angels, which,
high on the chancel arch,
seem to swim in air.

In God's love, I thought,
until, peering,
I saw that they are helmeted,
military guards with the job
of admitting some to heaven
and keeping others out.

Yet they were, too, figures
of energy, athletes
delighting in their element,
with a power the chiselled stone
still held after a thousand years.

Bullfinch on blackthorn

Alighting
on the trembling bough,
you are a firestorm
igniting the black, winter tree.

Bold bird,
today is all yours
and hers, with whom
you feed and mate and sing
flaming with joy.

Dawn: The Restless Earth

After Frances Hatch

Waves of colour
break on the shore.
　　　It is dawn
after millions of years –
　　　a moment
when the make of you
meets what comes to hand –

blackberry juice
　　　　　　　staining
the sketchbook page,
rainwater　　　mud
Otter sandstone

which remembers the desert,
torrents that drowned
an early reptile,

a bit broken
from Pangaea

　　　　　　　apparently
coming to rest
on this beach
at this hour
when you put in your hand

mixing the raw stuffs

with liquid yellow,
colour the sun makes
covering up
rifts & sandstorms & falls

leaving for now
this stillness
seething
in a deep pool
from which what rises
is something new –

                        a human word.

1 July 2016

Numbness descends
on our divisions
with the summer dark:
days sombre with rain
and cloud, as, in silence,
for two minutes, we are
at one thinking of them,
in fields of a Europe
torn apart, the old men
we knew, and the young
we did not – all their lives
in front of them, as
they fall away, and vanish,
undivided in the dark.

For a man who named his house *Mametz*

What can't be seen –

faces of friends
swimming up from the garden soil

bricks made of blood and clay
wire and splintered wood

a roof to hold off dreams

kindness a man chooses to live with
until he dies

Southwell Minster: Master of the Leaves

As leaves clutch
the capitals
        reaching up
As the columns
remember trees
        reaching down
so new life springs
still
        in shaped stone

So trace it back –
brother fire & sister water
working in the earth –
and a man
who does not know he is medieval,
a man who sees God alive
in the green world,
a master mason observing
in wood and copse and open field:
oak & maple
buttercup
hawthorn & vine
        each particular leaf
in the whole world no two the same

Trace the touch of his mind
on the trembling leaf

Feel the love
in his maker's fingers
as the stone springs alive.

Angel with nails

(Winchester Cathedral)

To David Gascoyne

An angel with yellow hair,
in blood spotted robe, holds
three great black nails.

No shipwright or carpenter
could fault them. With such nails
hammerbeams hold still;

where man of war or merchant
rotted, they are found.

These dwarf the angel's palm,
and also the handy cross.

This man below made the gift.
For seven centuries he kneels,
a shielded knight, and his wife
Anastasia kneels facing him.

They too were preserved,
borne on the painted wood.
Each square above them
pictures an act, but today

I see no Virgin or Saint,
no Christ in Majesty.
Only nails and an empty cross
draw me past tomb on tomb,

Colours of Empire,
disintegrating, dusty,
hang on the walls,
and while I sense

under monument, slab,
the fling of the nave,
something of worldly power
to weigh on me and force me

down, a worshipper of dust,
a workman's faultless nails
hold me here.
A world hangs on them.

Ancient buildings filled with light

for David Tress

1
To begin in the open:

on a pilgrim route
in a country of monodnock
and standing stone
where a painter crouches
huddled among gorse
against wind off the western sea…

And he too is peregrine,
a man with a vision
of colour, his senses
dyed in the stuff he works with…

He might have risen
from this earth
where foot has trodden on foot,
hooves struck sparks from rock

where through his hands
the ancient tower rises
daring the moor land's surge,
the sea thundering at the land's end.

2
Easter light fills the body of stone,
or a harvest of yellows and browns
spills bundles of wheat, the font
a cornucopia…

Walls that were bare for hundreds of years,
whitewash concealing the story
that once gave the building life,
blinding the Image of Pity,
now glow again
with yellow and gold of the natural day.

Only paint, but a man's work
with his life informing it,
his quick art which brushes aside
the fictions of the age,
the self locked in the skull,
the spiritless round of seasons and years.

Alone, he imagines
the breathing of the pews,
steps that have worn tracks
through the fields
and runnels in the stone floor,
a whisper of silent congregations.

Darkness will come as this day fades.
Until then he will work, open
to a freshness that quickens
the drab ribs of stone.

Somewhere, a blackbird

1
Open the door: the song
sounds at first like a word,
a lyrical word.

But this is not a word
we speak or can translate.

Where does it come from?
Not from the blackthorn
that is still without a flower.
From behind the fir, perhaps,
where magpies at their nest
taste blood in the song.

2
The words become a stream,
a musical stream.

But this is air, not water.
Spirit of air
with a freshness that blows in.

It opens a space in the mind.
It discovers a country
in the winter land.

I cannot explain what it means.
You have to open the door.

St Michael and All Angels, East Coker

'In my beginning is my end. Of your kindness,
pray for the soul of Thomas Stearns Eliot, poet.
In my end is my beginning.'

1
The request meets my eye with a shock.

I am disposed to pray.
But what should I pray for?

Is it an idea Plato would have known?
Or old Hamlet, the dead king
walking the battlements at Elsinore
until cockcrow?
Leaving before first light
touched sea and cold stone
he left to our imagination
some place we dread to think.

2
The book my first love gave me
was a paperback with a blue cover,
which she signed, with her wish
that the year before us would fulfil
all my ambitions. What a time it was,
that year, when, for us, everything fell apart.

In time, the book, too, disintegrated.
I replaced it with another – the same
and not the same – which I scarcely needed,
since the voice had entered into me, mixing
with the seasons of my mind and heart.

3

Surely there is matter in this ground,
dust and clay and bone,
leavings of generations, labourers
home from the open fields, lords
of the manor and men of god,
women and children, all of them,
the mighty and the meek. Here are histories
buried in Somerset clay, or absent ones,
remembered here, adventurers,
their tales written on stormy seas,
or in chronicles of a far land. We may imagine
St Michael and the Angels looking down.
Certainly, in this ground, the roots go deep.

4

What I see when I think of God
is a day breaking: cold, green light
spreading on hills beyond Gethsemane,
men asleep, and one awake, watching.
What he sees may be a light I have often thought of,
wondering what it means.
How it spreads, meeting the eyes of the man
who watches, who prays and watches
as the day, the astonishing day,
comes on remorselessly.

5

How it clutches at my heart
that old book with a blue cover
which fell apart in my hands.
How simple it seems sometimes
to know oneself
beyond all knowledge – the sense of it,
knowing what one does not know.

Words my friend wrote haunt me:
God sees us just as we are.

It was such a time: the love song
echoing in all things, colouring
the very air, remaking
the world around us, the Common
with its gorse flowering in every season,
the council estate and village streets,
Wainsford bridge and the stream
below stilled to a deep dark green.
Grasses in ditch and meadow
shone with an inner light.

Then it all fell apart, like the book,
but the words we spoke to each other,
like the words in the book, will live with me until I die.

I will ask
that God look kindly upon the soul
of Thomas Stearns Eliot, poet,
who entered our minds and hearts
when we were young, and lives with us,
and showed his humility by asking us to pray.

Homage to Charles Reznikoff

There is music
in this man walking.
Alone, he is one
with his kind,
a wanderer between
the old world and the new.
Solitary, in subways
and on sidewalks
he hears the song.
On streets of Manhattan,
by the Hudson River,
from Brooklyn
to Bronx, Bronx
to Brooklyn
and in Central Park,
his day's walk
is his vocation:
listener, composer,
new poet,
ancient scribe,
a wanderer who observes
fellow strangers,
pauses, writes
in his pocket book
and walks on, unknown,
minstrel at the feast
of common sights.

Talking with James Schuyler

Hearing your voice
it's the everyday real
that attracts: so, please,
could we talk? I think
we could have been friends,
so I see us sitting
together in a garden,
on Long Island
or an island off Maine
or West Wight,
some place homely
with summer flowers.
We talk about painters,
your friends or mine,
or John Constable's
'touches of white'
and 'sparkling air'.
Brushstrokes delight,
and quick words,
notations of diarists
we love, Thoreau
and White of Selborne,
Dorothy Wordsworth
teaching her brother
to see, all who, in this
prose age of public ruin
find, or make, 'an image
of life', who know what
we need are small things –
cell, or seed, or word
between friends, so,
please, could we talk?

Picture stone for Tomas Tranströmer

As the day darkens he travels north
sensing more than he can see
of pine forest, birches, lakes
where snow lies on the ice.

Boulders glimmer as the light fades.

*

Shape of a ship
preserved in sediment

spider & web caught
in Baltic amber:

the sea, also, is a maker
                            of images.

*

Rune-stone, boat, axe-head.
So the land is made.

In the poem, too,
beauty and pain twisted
together violently
form an intricate design.

*

Islands, mountains, forests
descending to the shore,
opening on Baltic inlets.

He works with the place that made him.

He makes a mark on the blank side of the stone.

An offering to Olav H. Hauge

How companionable
you are, solitary man!
Out in all seasons
to tend your trees,
returning to your desk
with aching back
and cracked hands
to write, or read Schopenhauer
or Emily Dickinson
or a Chinese poet
brief and wise as you,
then out again to prune
or graft, pick apples
or play scarecrow
to chase birds from the buds,
and with all, and through
all frost and sun and snow,
worker, watcher
of fjord and mountains:
a voice that comes
to us with offers tart and sweet
as your Norwegian fruit.

To Benjamin Fondane

Romania – Paris – Auschwitz

Singular man,
poet, philosopher,
passionate
Ulysses of the deep self,
wanderer on seas
known and unknown,
wildly alive –
rhythm & beat
of body blood nerves
mind & spirit:
Benjamin Fondane,
when the Reich has lain
a thousand years in the dust
your voice will speak
not for your self alone
but for the millions
        each living soul.

Daughter of Earth

for Liz Mathews

1
You receive,
and what you receive
you give back.

2
You take raw stuff,
found materials,
and make a shape.

Clay becomes a vessel
in your hands, a form
that speaks of you
and of the Earth,
the sky, the elemental fire.

3
What the Thames brings you –
a driftwood stick –
you use to form letters,
letters that make words,
words that bring to light
the poem as it forms:

a gift received
a gift revealed.

Still-life for Rutger Kopland

It is what you show us:
this spirit alive
in the sandy heath
of Drenthe, mist rising to reveal
a windmill, sails motionless,
a rhine in a field of blue clay
that remembers the sea.
A grey heron poised at the brink.

What you show us is poet's work,
a lowlands of the mind,
a country broken from the husk of the given world.
Somewhere you knew once
when you were a child, and never forgot.
It came to you with words
that forever recall the pasture
behind the pasture, and water
so still it trembles with another life.

Christopher's birds

'there is beauty in birds and all about them'
                    Christopher Middleton

Man of the sun,
dancer,
whose each step
was, brilliantly,
a surprise,
I could not
write for you
a dirge, or match
your colours
or lore of birds
of foreign climes –
hummingbird
or parrot, condor
or kingbird or loon –
so I call up
an image hoping
it may suffice:
a charm of finches
in a waste
of thistles, which
as they dance
from plant to plant
bring down the sun
with flashes of red,
and black and gold.

Epstein's Lazarus

1
Chisel and rasp
hand and brain and soul,
the weight of the work appals.
Sweating, the sculptor
embraces the stone.
        Matter must give.
He is all muscle, Hercules
of imaginative force.
        Matter must yield
and the worked stone live.

2
At a leap
Lazarus the dervish
will throw off these bonds,
stone man become flesh.

The effort makes him giddy.
His mind spins, his thoughts
are a desert storm.

Martha and Mary wait,
almost fainting,
while his friend works
the miracle with a word.

Soon, Lazarus will emerge
from the four-day dark.
His tortured feet
will feel once more
the dust of Bethany.
He will walk rejoicing,
kicking up sand on the path

he is blind to, which
leads to the second death.

Soon, he will breathe.

In Memory of Stephen Batty

Wasted, unable to move,
he remembers being young,
a priest fresh in the faith
that is his life, when
he stood on a chair
in a chapel to sketch
a triptych of the fifteenth century:
The Raising of Lazarus.

Something not meant to be there
caught his eye: the husk
of a woodlouse
on a corner of the picture.

How it breathed at the edge
of meaning, this fellow creature
of dust. Surely, he asks,
where would we be if this
were not chosen to live again
in some damp spot,
its proper home
under bark of a tree in paradise?

At Time's Edge

In memory of Anne Cluysenaar

1
Seeking words to speak of you
I hear you say: *'where*
we are both strangers and at home'.

I respond, and expect you to answer.
I listen, and the silence, like a sea
gone far out, reverberates
leadenly with a memory of sound.

> *Fire lips*
> *water*
> *as the day dies*

2
Searching for news of you
I stumble on a photograph
taken in a Somerset farmyard:
Ministry of Information, 1944.

You are standing with your parents,
artists in exile. A donkey
is nuzzling your father's hand.
A goose and a hen pick in the mud
around your feet.
How solid you are,
what a sturdy little girl
with a mass of blond hair:
the poet at nine years of age.

> *Fire quickens*
> *touching*
> *the water's skin*

3
It is the moment that holds you
and where you are, in wartime
at this English farm, you are
in a place no one can see:
                    a border
between languages and countries.
At this edge, you are
already, in your way, the stranger
you taught me, in my way, to know myself.

Blood-lipped
a wave seethes
kissing the shore

4
Dare I speak aloud
what I say to myself:
dear soul, dear fellow pilgrim?

Will the language we hear
around us bear such words?
'If breath is not spirit,
what is it for?'
I hear you ask.

Snakes of fire
ride in
with the tide

5
What I see is you
with your whole life –
not finished, but like a sea
that has heaved up against a wall.

It is the self you knew as process:
tides, currents, depths.

And in the depths life glimpsed
or unknown, but generative,
the creative source you knew as a child.

> *Water covers prints*
> *first light*
> *will expose*

6
Wales became your home,
the depth of time exposed
in rock fall and quarry face,
the first footprint on an ancient beach,
the labyrinthine forest paths
and sheep walks, ways
of poet and healer, and ever
the green and shadowed places
of Wentwood Forest, the Beacons
and Black Mountains
and valley of the river Usk.

It became your home
because you did not claim it,
but knew yourself a wanderer
in and out of languages, and between
countries, along the edge of time.

> *The night,*
> *the black night,*
> *shivers with stars*

7
A true poet, your life is still to come
in other minds: the life embodied
in your words, a life's work,
quick and shining, which helps
other strangers to know themselves.

Reading Anne's last poems

1
In old age, you were still
a child of time – deep time:
reader of original forms,
and strange forms that may be.
You touched with fellow feeling
the hand on the cave wall,
the auroch and the wild horse,
as you rode your cob at Wentwood Farm
or fed the chickens and the sheep.

You reached back,
far back, past human words
to matter and the first cell.
Life to you was one
and wonderfully many:
time past, time present
and to come –
all creative flux.

2
Self, too, is a step from the river
that flows through us all, as it runs
under and through your poems –
rivers, streams, lakes, the sea.
Words move on its surface, language
appears from the depths –
you are a child with your parents,
a young woman, an old woman,
at each instant yourself and a stranger
meeting the life you are part of,
knowing what you do not know
but sensing the river as it moves,
the loops and pools, bridges,
islands, each with its partial view.

3
Finally, these poems
were fragments, cut short,
as you knew we and all our works are,
yet speaking of and beyond you
and quick with your being to the last.

Green rain

Remembering Les Arnold

1
Once you told me
you didn't trust a slow driver.

You were fast –
        driving, writing, teaching
with energy, awakening
in others their creative life,
and quick to leave us.

One day the man
most alive, the next
        gone.

2
I sat over your papers
on a cold, wet morning
in April,
        rain on the window
reflected leafing trees –

this flesh of the world!

I sat at your desk
with your words for company:

        work-in-progress:

quick notations,
poems half-finished,
a story for children
about a red bus.

Looking up, I expected
to see you dashing past.

But of course there was no one.
Only rain drops
        in green light, moving
slowly down the window pane.

At a Requiem Mass

In memory of Jim Insole

With the words of the priests,
with their movements,
in front of the coffin,
under the holy images,
I find myself,
now here, now there,
walking with you, treading
again in the steps of a lifetime.

I recall the shell
that I keep on my desk,
a small, white bivalve,
boat shaped
in which you drew
an anchor and wrote:
'Mother Bank IOW 1994'
and, below,
MARIA ASSUMPTA.

How much of your life
this little thing contains.

*

Anyone who desires faith
will receive it, you said.

Forgive me –
as you always did –
this splinter of unbelief.

The way I have taken
is uncertain as a cliff path,

or a track disappearing,
where the trees close in.

*

A green woodpecker crosses a glade,
laughing.
Our path, along
the disused railway track,
leads into the woods.

All around us fungi
are busy at their work.
We walk on, deeper in,
talking and talking.

*

Our steps trace
a maze of paths.
We walk in hoof marks
of Forest ponies,
in oakwoods, where they say
Rufus was slain,
on Jutish heath
where a Scots pine
twisted by sea wind
stands, as if the world
were made for loneliness,
along the shore
where the shingle drifts.

*

When you played and sang
there was magic
in common things.

It was an enchanted world
you played and sang into being.

I think of the mandolin
with no one to cradle it,
coffined in its box.

We are the singers today
and you the silent one.

*

They speak of your face
shining in welcome at death.

It was not another world
you lived in, but this one
as it truly is, constantly renewed
by the Bread and Wine.

*

On Barton beach
after a night of scrumpy
and song we walk into
a hangover morning,
the Island extinguished
in mist, unshrouding
like a dream,
washed shingle
at our feet, gleaming,
gold in the sunburst.
This ancient world,
cliffs eroding, slides
of blue clay, from which
you made goblets for wine
and beads for a rosary.

What is the world unless
the world that's given
in friendship and in love.

*

Light where imagination
fails, perpetual,
without shadow,
where I envisage you
walking away, vanishing
in eternal welcome.

So I hope, restless
with spoken words
that draw me back
to the sound of our steps
scrunching dead leaves
or shingle at the sea's edge.

*

At Oxey, tide out
and a smell of mud and salt
in the creek. Beyond the seawall
the Solent glittering.
For me, this was a place
always on the brink
of revelation.

For you, God
was everywhere.

If everywhere, then here –
where the river surges,
turbid and brown with autumn rain,
acorns falling

around us as we walk
further in, talking and talking.

*

The moon of the High Street clock
will see other revellers home.

Other minstrels will pluck
their mandolins, and lift their voices
against the shush of the sea,
other poets fumble for words.
Friends will walk the shore
or sit out on the shingle
talking of other times.

Waves will break,
tides will turn,
the Island appear
and vanish in mist.

Songs will be sung,
words spoken.

But never again your songs,
never again our words.

*

A green woodpecker crosses a glade.

Silence falls
after the echo of its laughing call.
The only sound is distant voices,
where we have disappeared among the trees.

Notes

Word and Stone
The image of 'A carved hand/holding a cross/...cut in the castle floor' originated with the picture of such a cross set in the floor of Yarmouth Castle, Isle of Wight, reproduced in Jude James, *Hurst Castle: An Illustrated History*, The Dovecote Press, 1986.

In the Lloyd George Museum
The Welsh poet, Gwenallt (David Gwenallt Jones, 1899–1968), is the subject of this poem. I have been trying for many years to write a poem honouring Gwenallt. My first effort, 'To a Welsh Poet', appeared in *The Elements* in 1972. The third section of 'Writer's Workshop', *Adamah*, 2002, was a more substantial attempt. 'In the Lloyd George Museum' incorporates elements of these poems, especially the second. It is, however, a complete reworking of the materials. For information about Gwenallt and his poetry, I owe a special debt to A. M. Allchin, D. Densil Morgan, and Patrick Thomas, *Sensuous Glory: The Poetic Vision of D. Gwenallt Jones*, Canterbury Press, 2000.

Wood Fidley Rain
'An old book' refers to J. R. Wise's *The New Forest, its History and Scenery*, 1863.

From Wordsworth on Epitaphs
Some words in the final verse paragraph quote Wordsworth's 'Essay upon Epitaphs', Paul M. Zall (ed.), *Literary Criticism of William Wordsworth*, University of Nebraska Press, 1966.

St Michael and All Angels, East Coker
'Some words my friend wrote': 'God in His pure Presence reveals to us just what we really are', Gerard Casey, *Night Horizons*, Phudd Bottom Press, 1997.

Talking with James Schuyler
The Diaries of James Schuyler, Black Sparrow Press, 1997, is the source of the phrases in quotation marks.

To Benjamin Fondane
I read Fontane's thought as a form of Christian existentialism, in which defence of the value of the person is universal, and defies History's obliterating force.

Reading Anne's Last Poems
I wrote this poem after writing the Foreword to Anne Cluysenaar's 'Last Poems', which remains unpublished to date.

Acknowledgements

St Laurence's Bradford on Avon is a new version of a section from *Arnolds Wood*, Flarestack, 2005.

Picture-stone for Tomas Tranströmer revises the poem that first appeared in *Our Lady of Europe*, Enitharmon Press, 1997.

Angel with Nails is a new version of a poem that was first published in *For David Gascoyne on his sixty-fifth birthday*, Enitharmon Press, 1981.

Green Rain was incorporated in my essay, 'Beginnings', *A Place in Words: 25 Years of Creative Writing at Bath Spa University*, Bath Spa University Press, 2017.

At Time's Edge was my contribution to the book of that title, containing work in memory of Anne Cluysenaar, published by The Vaughan Association in 2016.

Other poems first appeared in *Agenda*, *Planet*, *Red Poets*, and *Shearsman*. I thank the editors of these publications.

I owe so much to Mieke, my late wife, including her keen sense of whether a poem works or not, and where it belongs in a sequence.

I am grateful to my friend, Christopher Meredith, for his critical readings of versions of these poems, and to Deborah Price for making me a fair copy of the text.